THIS BLOG PLANNER BELONGS TO

CONTACT DETAILS

MY BLOG IDEAS
MIND MAP

MY BLOG IDEAS

SUBJECT

IDEAS

PICTURES/GRAPHICS

ROUGH DRAFT

NOTES

OTHER

MY BLOG IDEAS
MIND MAP

MY BLOG IDEAS

SUBJECT

IDEAS

PICTURES/GRAPHICS

ROUGH DRAFT

NOTES

OTHER

MY BLOG IDEAS
MIND MAP

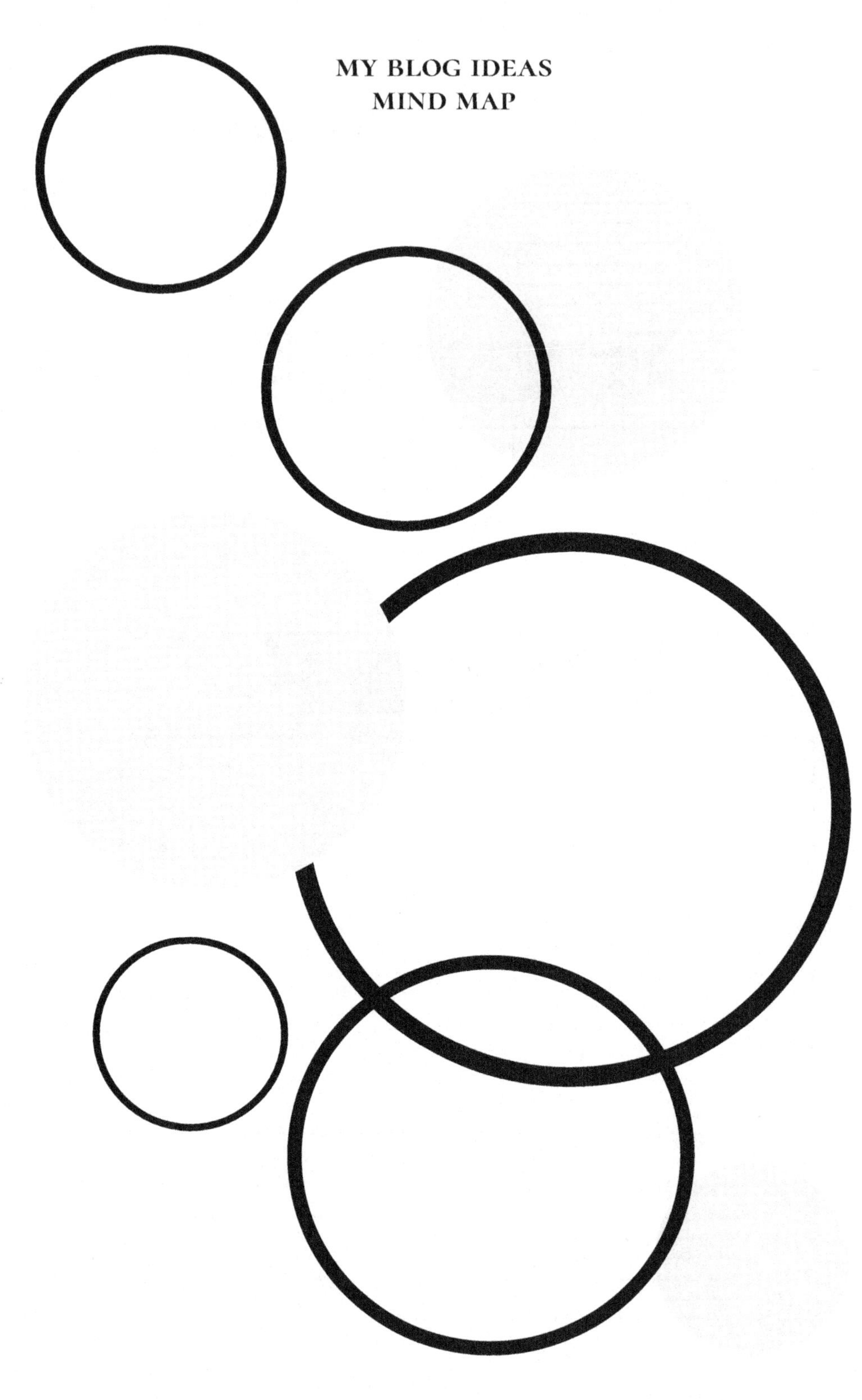

MY BLOG IDEAS

SUBJECT

IDEAS

PICTURES/GRAPHICS

ROUGH DRAFT

NOTES

OTHER

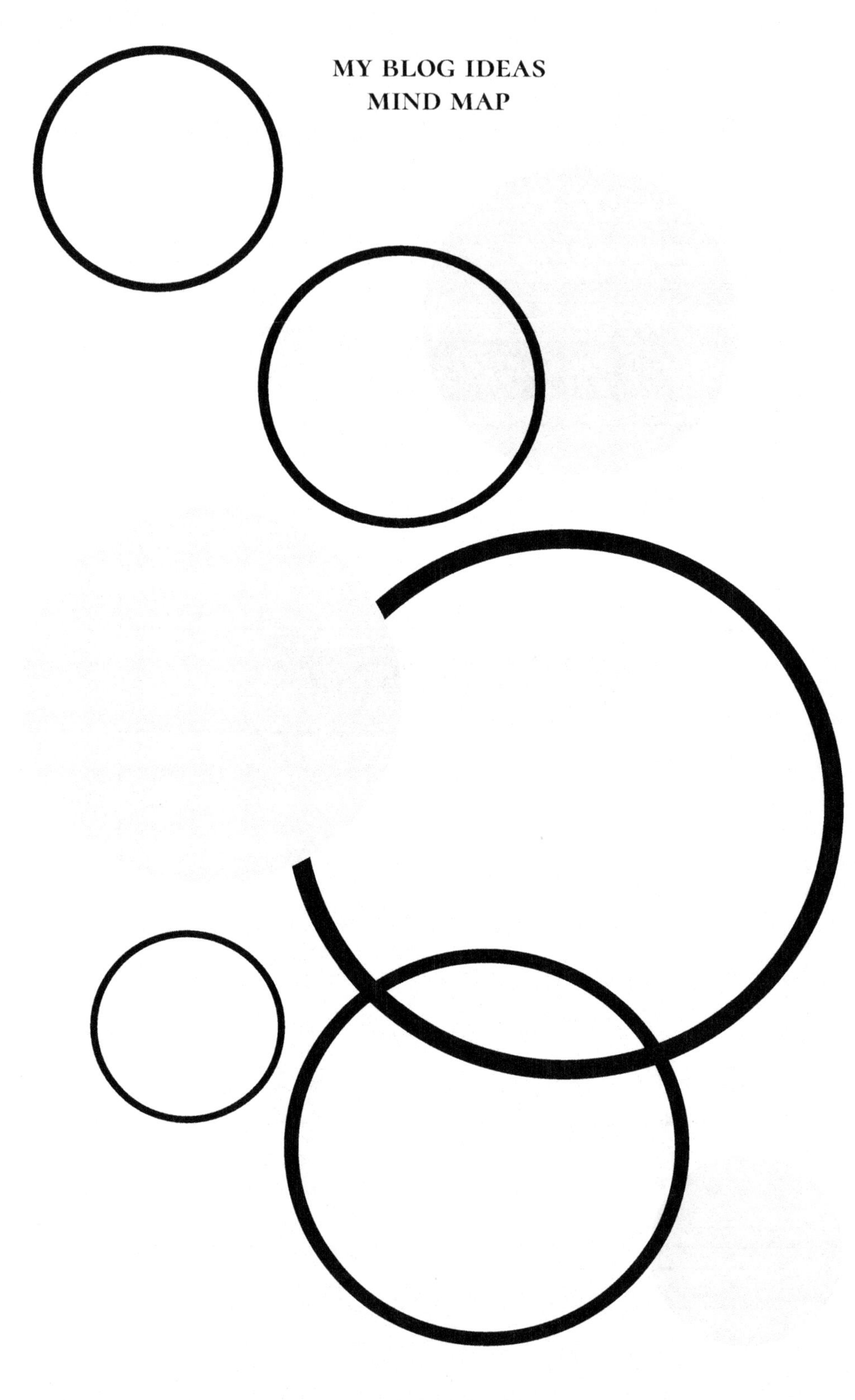
MY BLOG IDEAS
MIND MAP

MY BLOG IDEAS

SUBJECT

IDEAS

PICTURES/GRAPHICS

ROUGH DRAFT

NOTES

OTHER

MY BLOG IDEAS MIND MAP

MY BLOG IDEAS

SUBJECT

IDEAS

PICTURES/GRAPHICS

ROUGH DRAFT

NOTES

OTHER

MY BLOG IDEAS
MIND MAP

MY BLOG IDEAS

SUBJECT

IDEAS

PICTURES/GRAPHICS

ROUGH DRAFT

NOTES

OTHER

MY BLOG IDEAS
MIND MAP

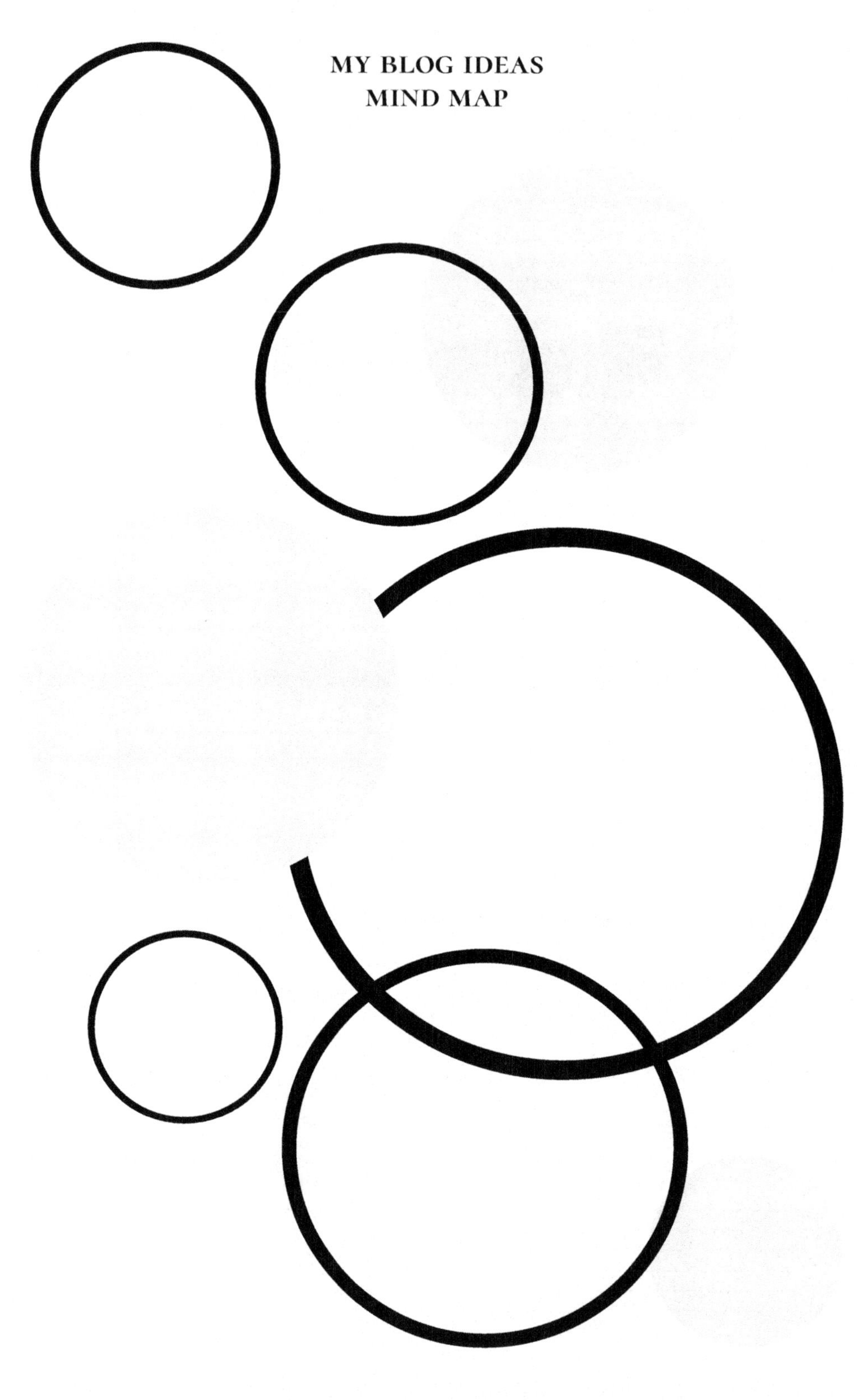

MY BLOG IDEAS

SUBJECT

IDEAS

PICTURES/GRAPHICS

ROUGH DRAFT

NOTES

OTHER

MY BLOG IDEAS MIND MAP

MY BLOG IDEAS

SUBJECT

IDEAS

PICTURES/GRAPHICS

ROUGH DRAFT

NOTES

OTHER

MY BLOG IDEAS MIND MAP

MY BLOG IDEAS

SUBJECT

IDEAS

PICTURES/GRAPHICS

ROUGH DRAFT

NOTES

OTHER

MY BLOG IDEAS MIND MAP

MY BLOG IDEAS

SUBJECT

IDEAS

PICTURES/GRAPHICS

ROUGH DRAFT

NOTES

OTHER

MY BLOG IDEAS MIND MAP

MY BLOG IDEAS

SUBJECT

IDEAS

PICTURES/GRAPHICS

ROUGH DRAFT

NOTES

OTHER

MY BLOG IDEAS
MIND MAP

MY BLOG IDEAS

SUBJECT

IDEAS

PICTURES/GRAPHICS

ROUGH DRAFT

NOTES

OTHER

MY BLOG IDEAS MIND MAP

MY BLOG IDEAS

SUBJECT

IDEAS

PICTURES/GRAPHICS

ROUGH DRAFT

NOTES

OTHER

MY BLOG IDEAS
MIND MAP

MY BLOG IDEAS

SUBJECT

IDEAS

PICTURES/GRAPHICS

ROUGH DRAFT

NOTES

OTHER

MY BLOG IDEAS MIND MAP

MY BLOG IDEAS

SUBJECT

IDEAS

PICTURES/GRAPHICS

ROUGH DRAFT

NOTES

OTHER

MY BLOG IDEAS MIND MAP

MY BLOG IDEAS

SUBJECT

IDEAS

PICTURES/GRAPHICS

ROUGH DRAFT

NOTES

OTHER

MY BLOG IDEAS MIND MAP

MY BLOG IDEAS

SUBJECT

IDEAS

PICTURES/GRAPHICS

ROUGH DRAFT

NOTES

OTHER

MY BLOG IDEAS
MIND MAP

MY BLOG IDEAS

SUBJECT

IDEAS

PICTURES/GRAPHICS

ROUGH DRAFT

NOTES

OTHER

MY BLOG IDEAS
MIND MAP

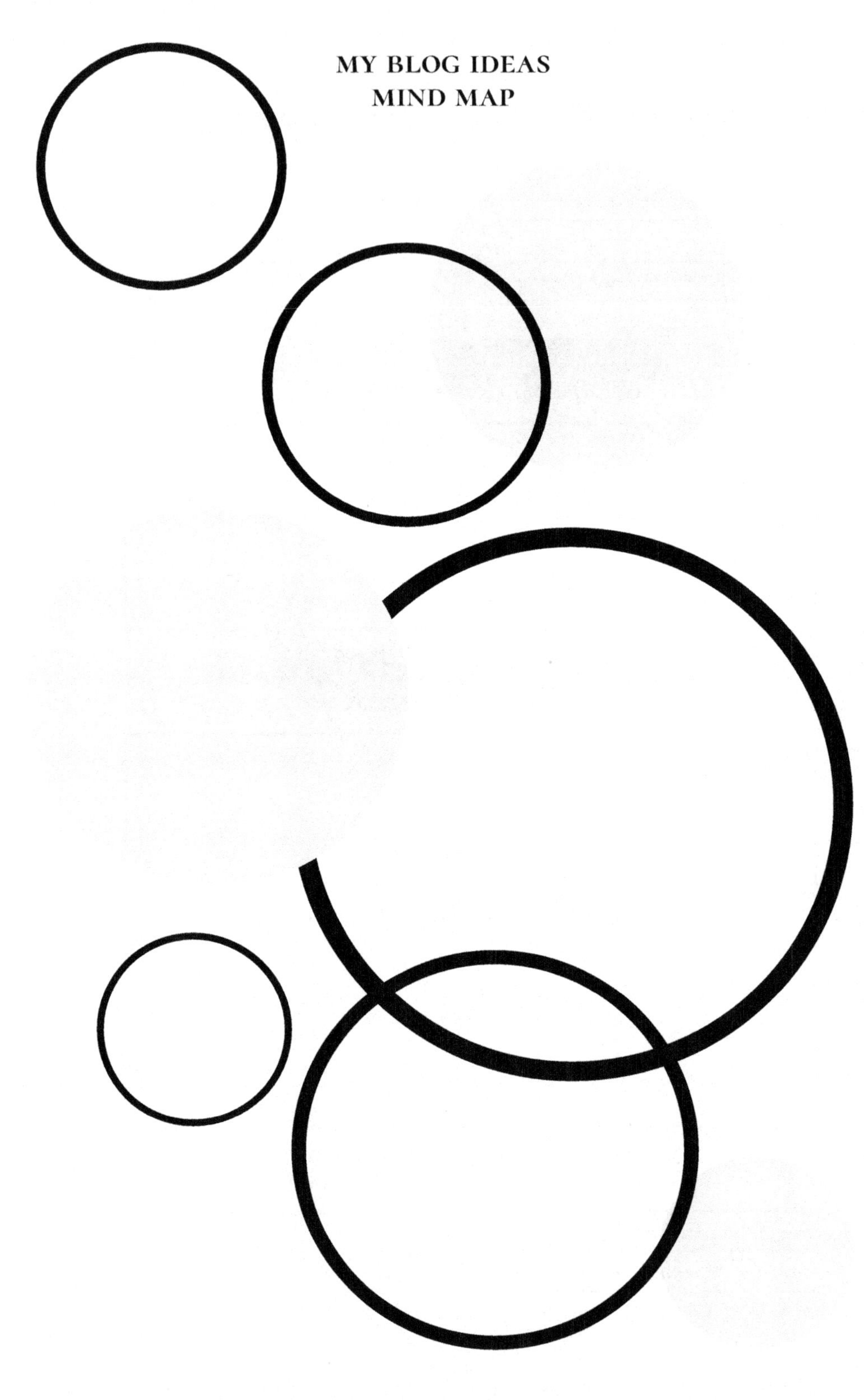

MY BLOG IDEAS

SUBJECT

IDEAS

PICTURES/GRAPHICS

ROUGH DRAFT

NOTES

OTHER

MY BLOG IDEAS
MIND MAP

MY BLOG IDEAS

SUBJECT

IDEAS

PICTURES/GRAPHICS

ROUGH DRAFT

NOTES

OTHER

MY BLOG IDEAS MIND MAP

MY BLOG IDEAS

SUBJECT

IDEAS

PICTURES/GRAPHICS

ROUGH DRAFT

NOTES

OTHER

MY BLOG IDEAS MIND MAP

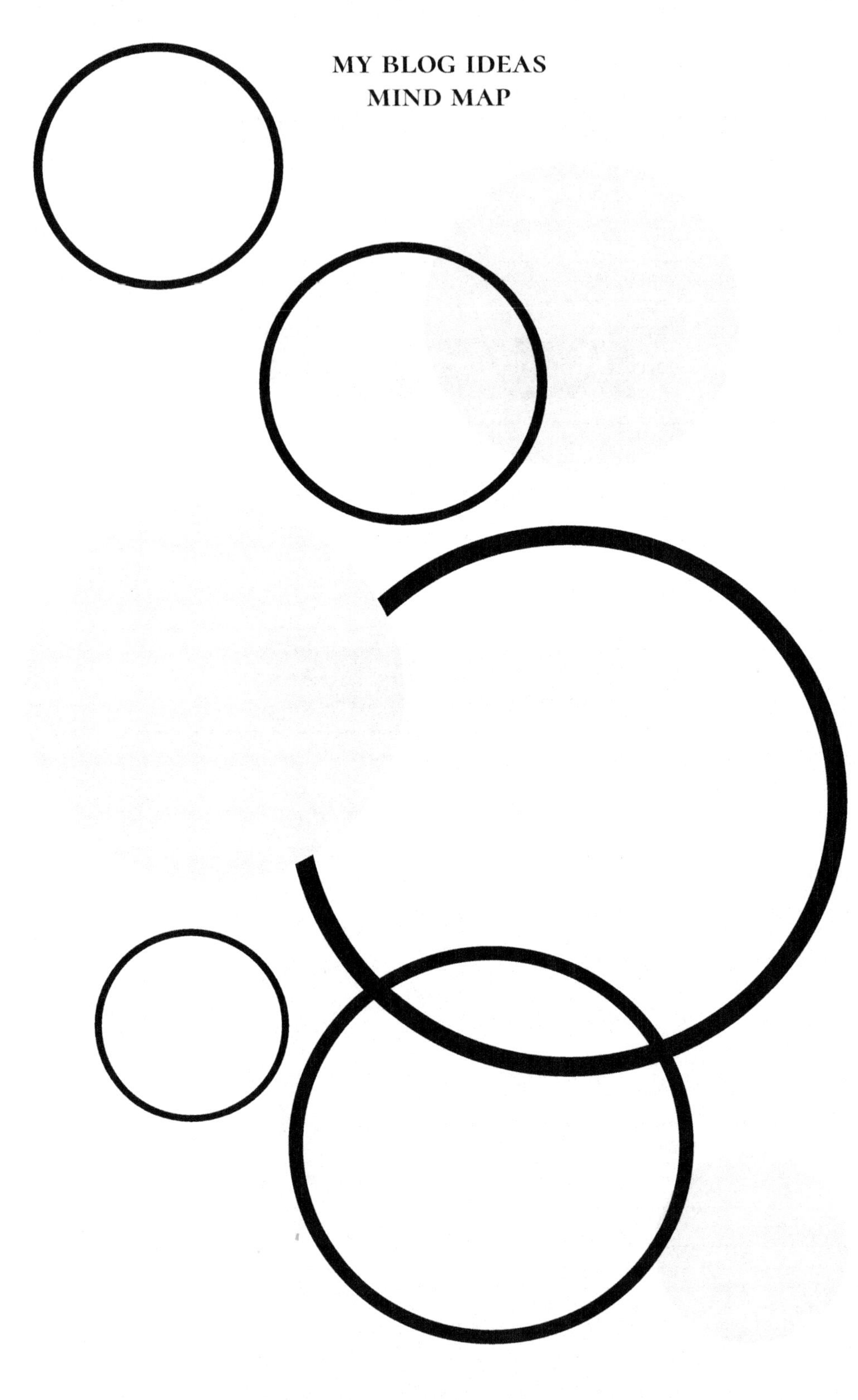

MY BLOG IDEAS

SUBJECT

IDEAS

PICTURES/GRAPHICS

ROUGH DRAFT

NOTES

OTHER

MY BLOG IDEAS
MIND MAP

MY BLOG IDEAS

SUBJECT

IDEAS

PICTURES/GRAPHICS

ROUGH DRAFT

NOTES

OTHER

MY BLOG IDEAS MIND MAP

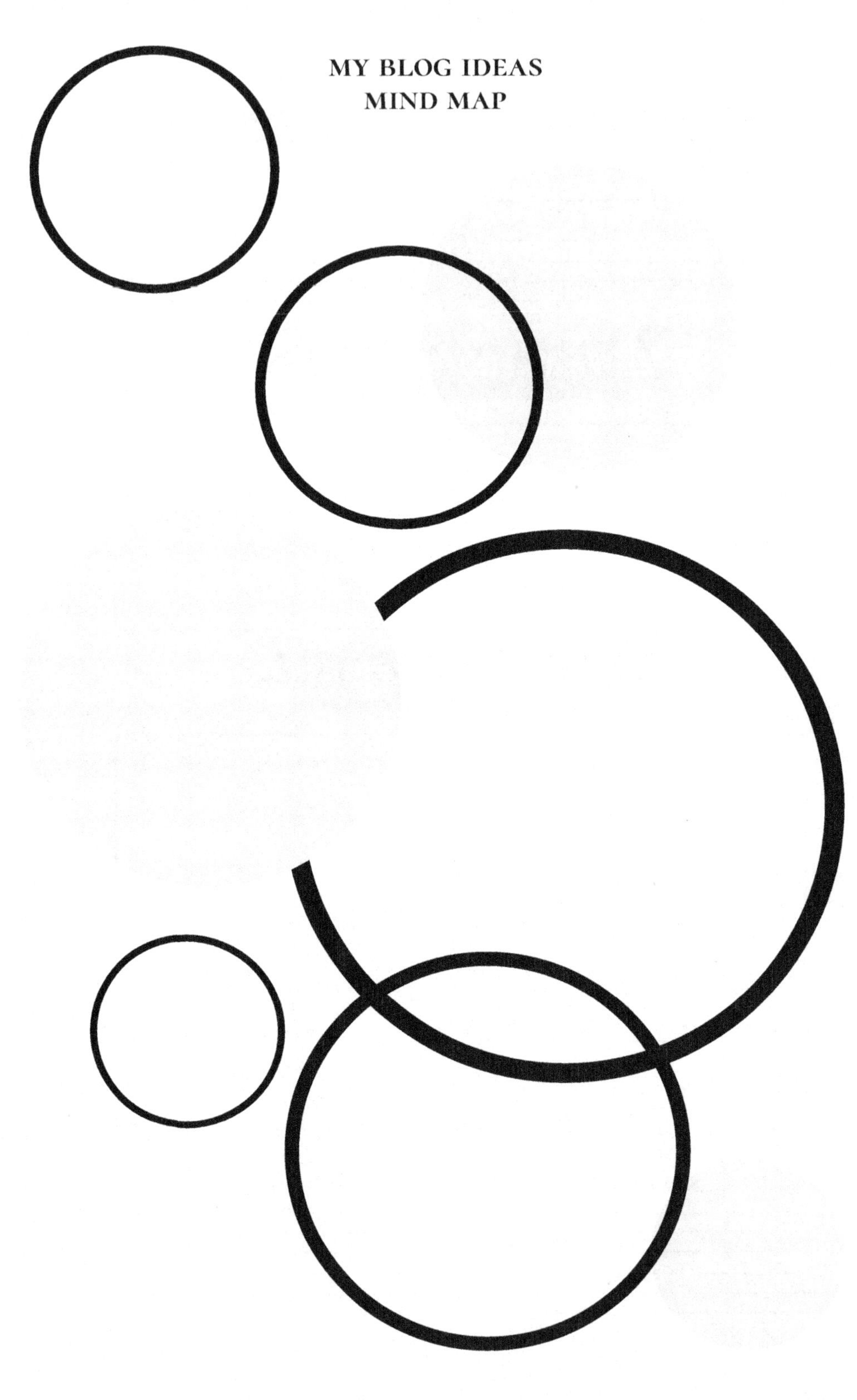

MY BLOG IDEAS

SUBJECT

IDEAS

PICTURES/GRAPHICS

ROUGH DRAFT

NOTES

OTHER

MY BLOG IDEAS MIND MAP

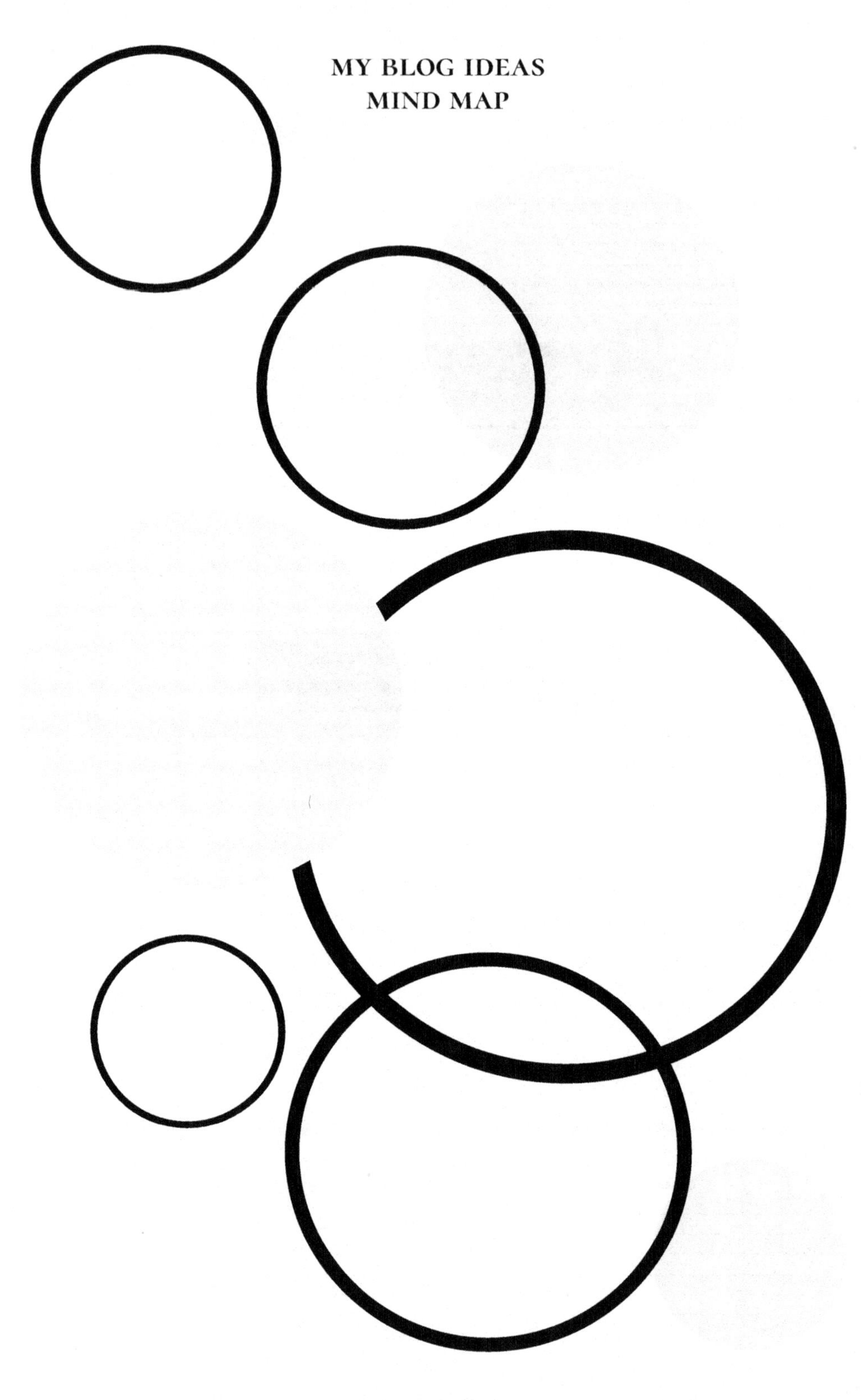

MY BLOG IDEAS

SUBJECT

IDEAS

PICTURES/GRAPHICS

ROUGH DRAFT

NOTES

OTHER

MY BLOG IDEAS
MIND MAP

MY BLOG IDEAS

SUBJECT

IDEAS

PICTURES/GRAPHICS

ROUGH DRAFT

NOTES

OTHER

MY BLOG IDEAS MIND MAP

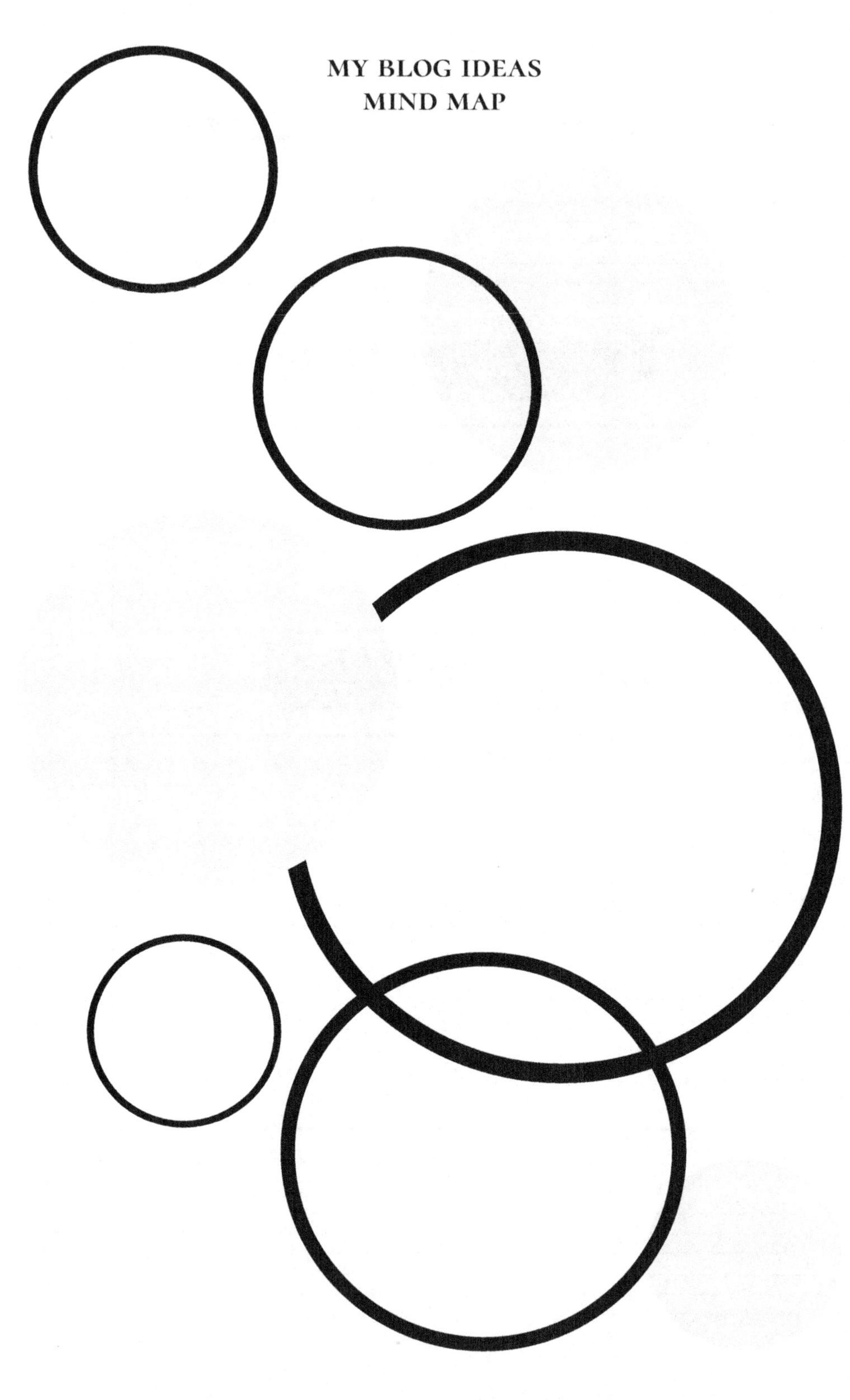

MY BLOG IDEAS

SUBJECT

IDEAS

PICTURES/GRAPHICS

ROUGH DRAFT

NOTES

OTHER

MY BLOG IDEAS
MIND MAP

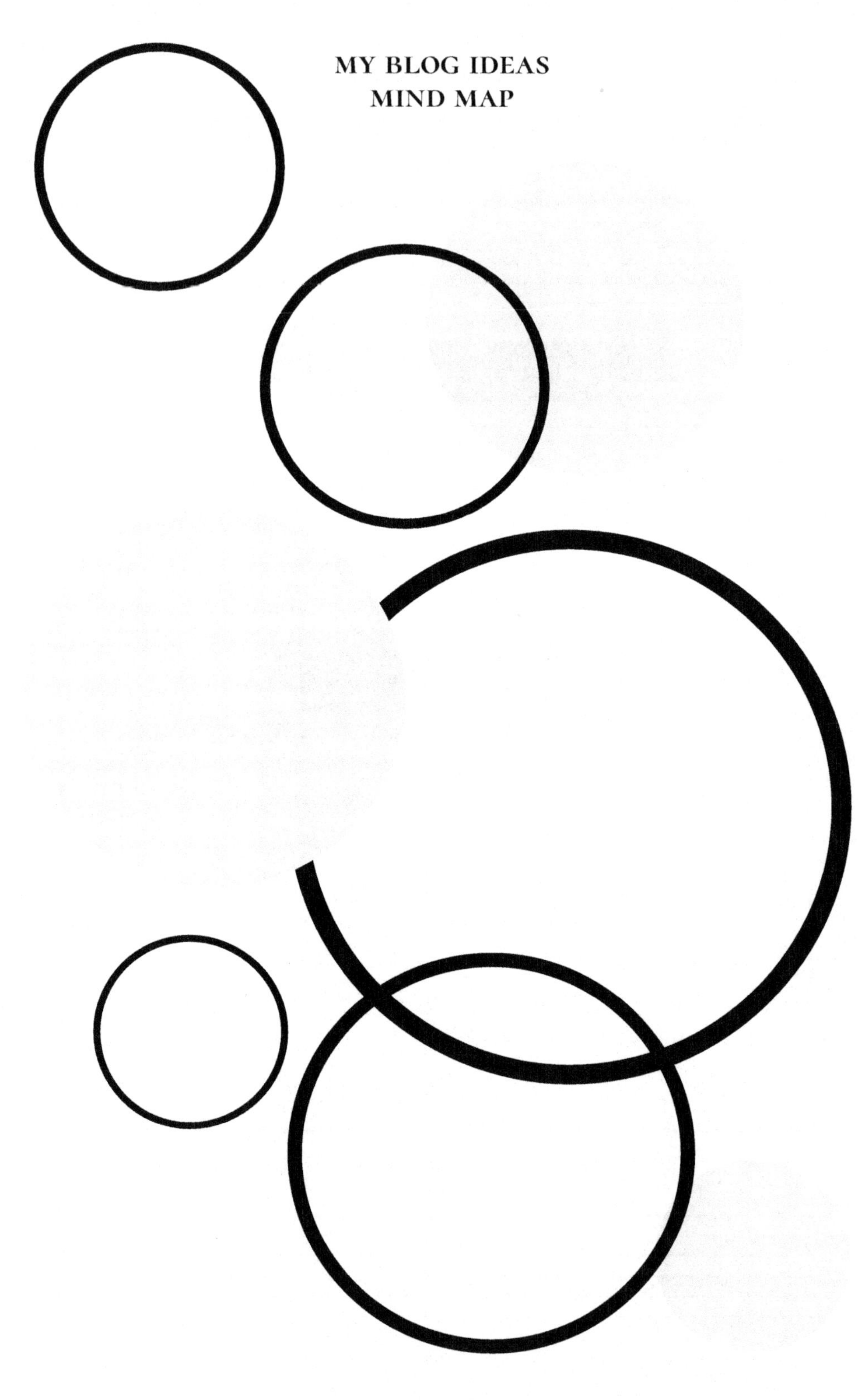

MY BLOG IDEAS

SUBJECT

IDEAS

PICTURES/GRAPHICS

ROUGH DRAFT

NOTES

OTHER

MY BLOG IDEAS MIND MAP

MY BLOG IDEAS

SUBJECT

IDEAS

PICTURES/GRAPHICS

ROUGH DRAFT

NOTES

OTHER

MY BLOG IDEAS MIND MAP

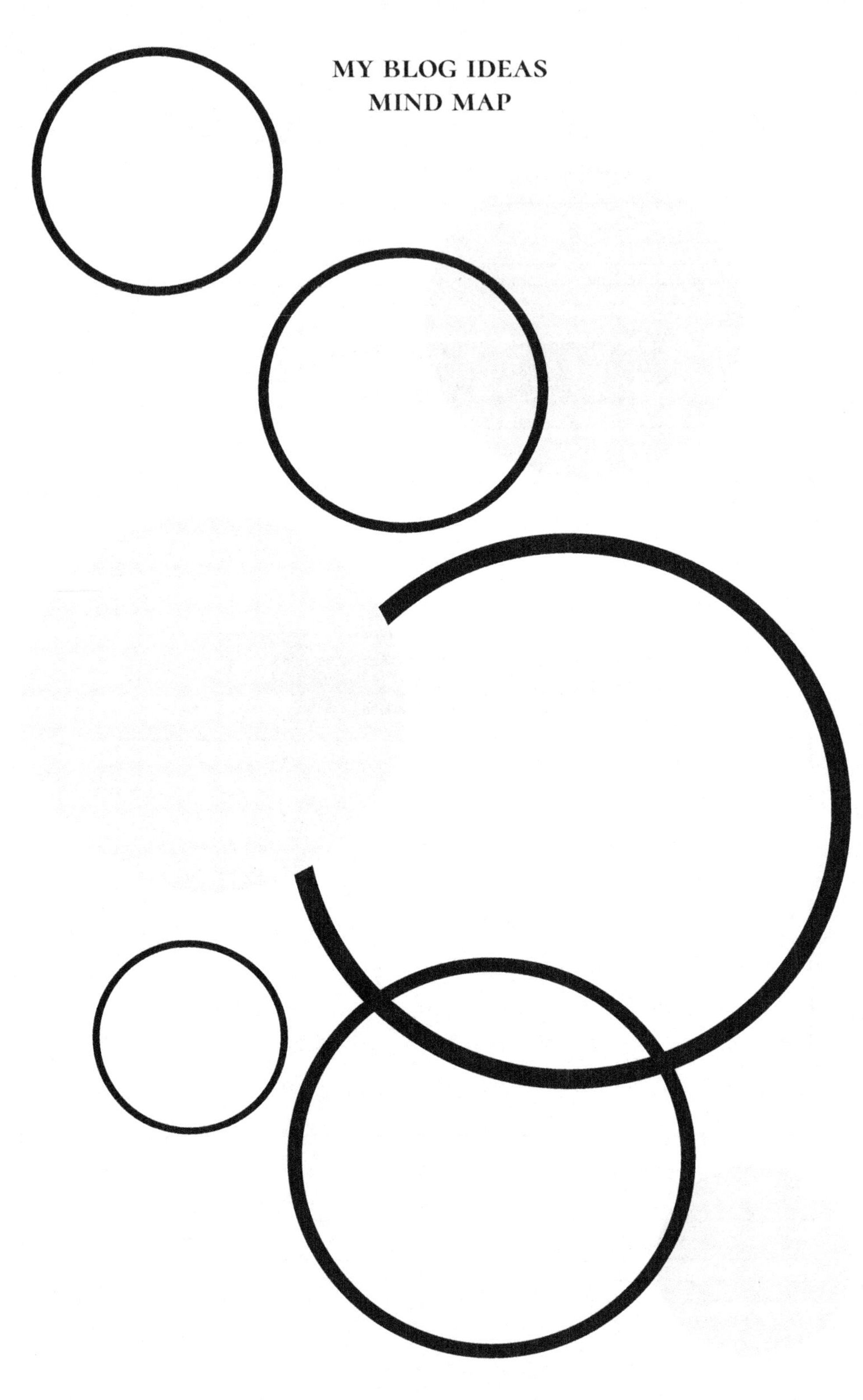

MY BLOG IDEAS

SUBJECT

IDEAS

PICTURES/GRAPHICS

ROUGH DRAFT

NOTES

OTHER

MY BLOG IDEAS
MIND MAP

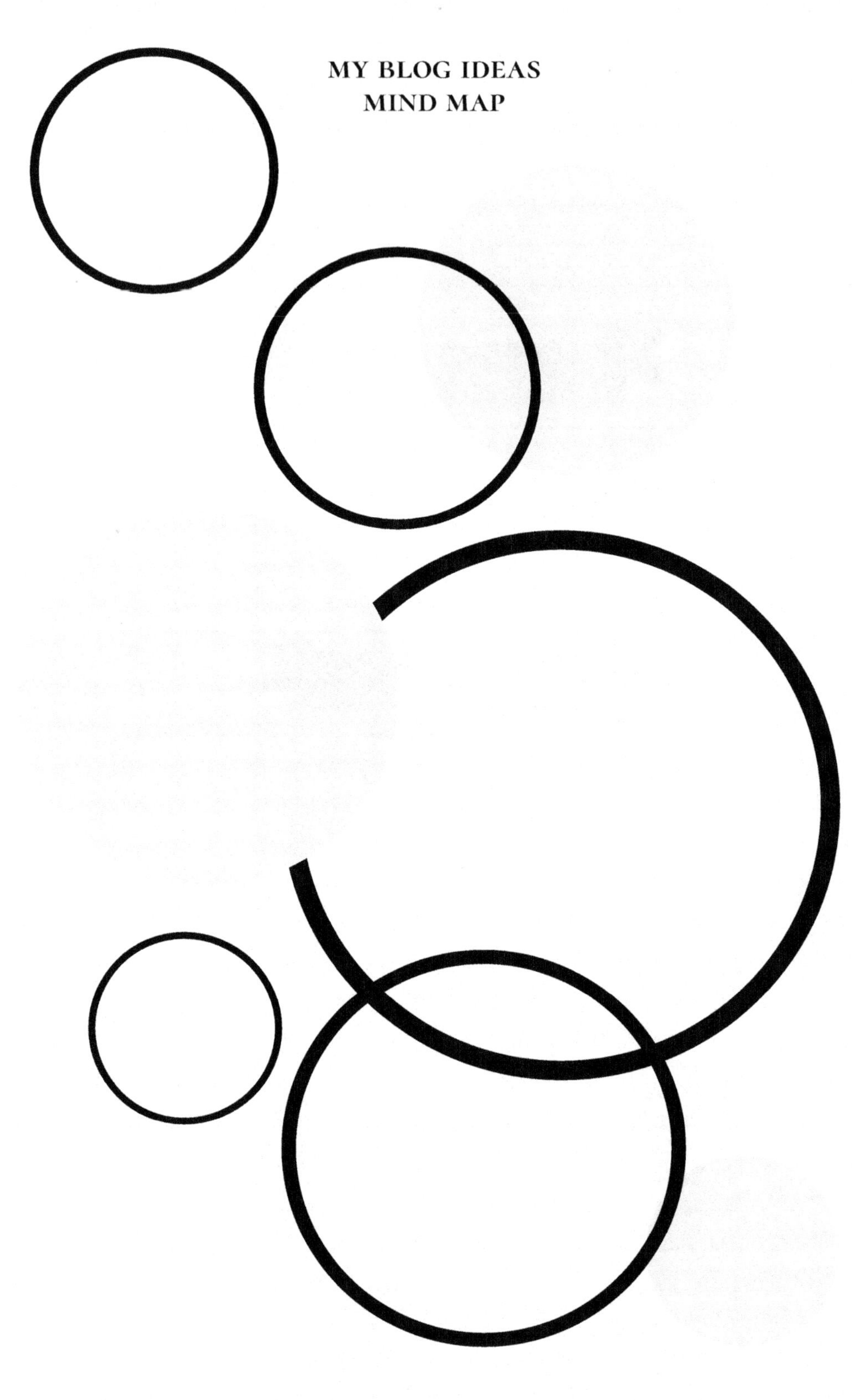

MY BLOG IDEAS

SUBJECT

IDEAS

PICTURES/GRAPHICS

ROUGH DRAFT

NOTES

OTHER

MY BLOG IDEAS
MIND MAP

MY BLOG IDEAS

SUBJECT

IDEAS

PICTURES/GRAPHICS

ROUGH DRAFT

NOTES

OTHER

MY BLOG IDEAS MIND MAP

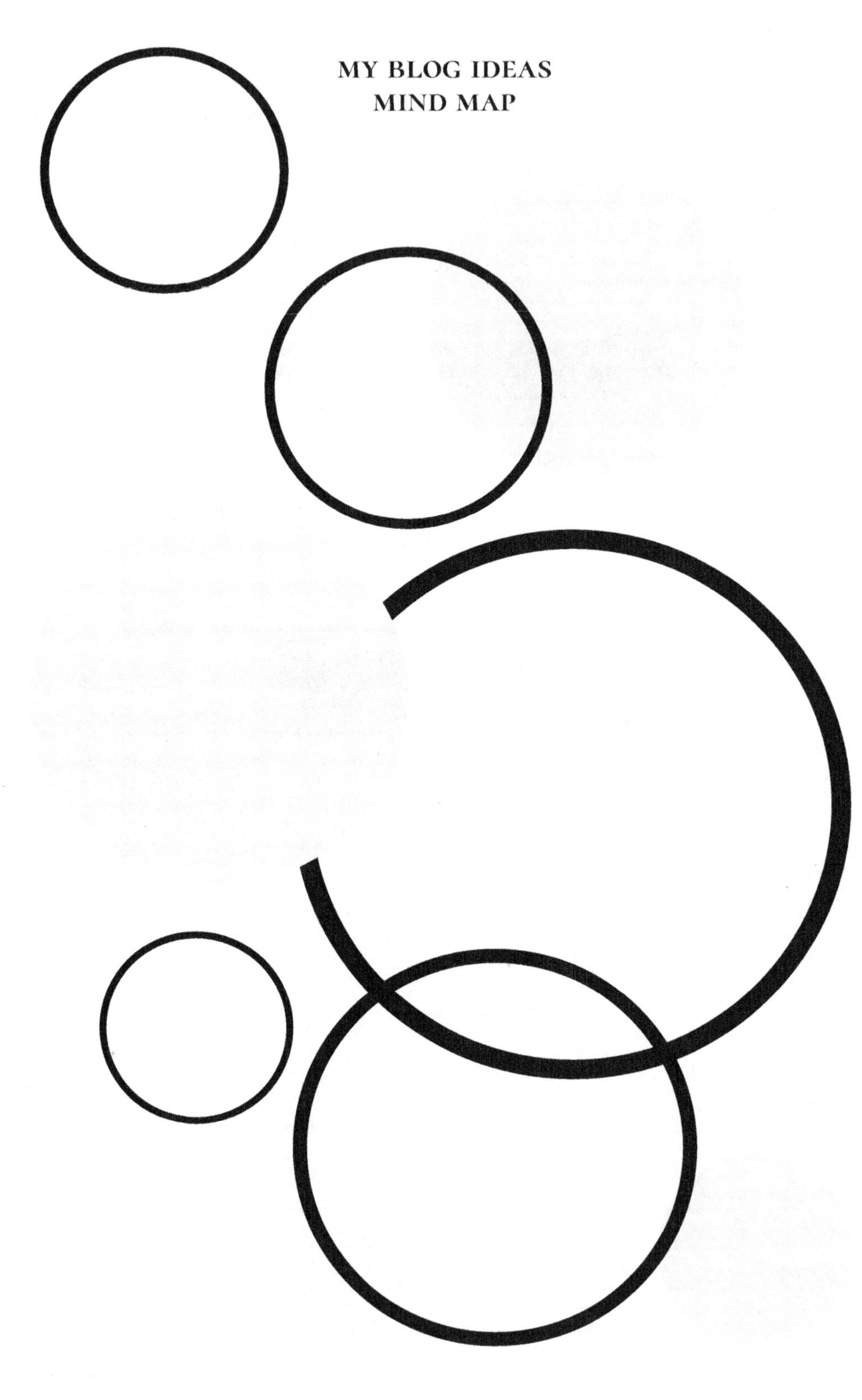

MY BLOG IDEAS

SUBJECT

IDEAS

PICTURES/GRAPHICS

ROUGH DRAFT

NOTES

OTHER

MY BLOG IDEAS MIND MAP

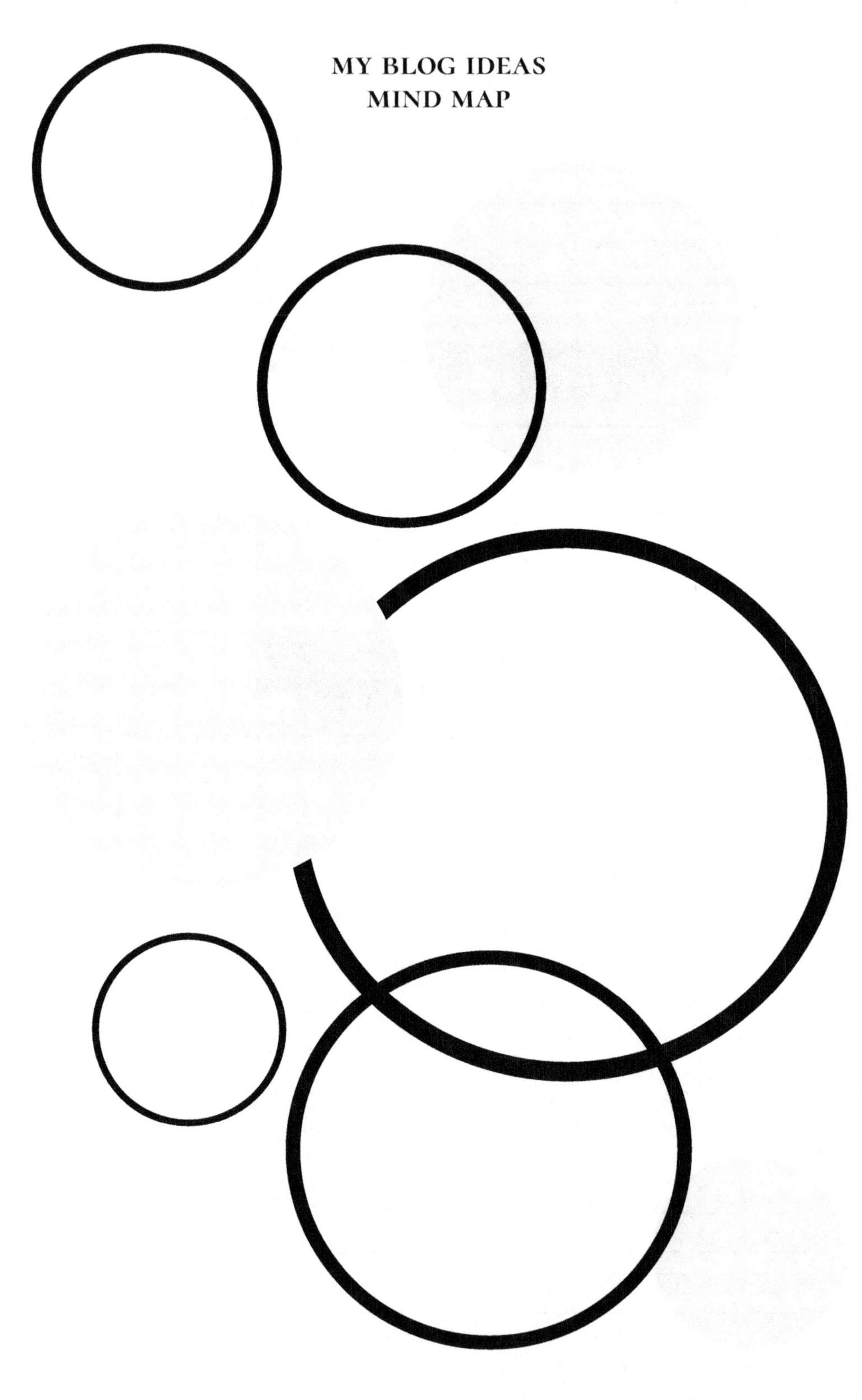

MY BLOG IDEAS

SUBJECT

IDEAS

PICTURES/GRAPHICS

ROUGH DRAFT

NOTES

OTHER

MY BLOG IDEAS MIND MAP

MY BLOG IDEAS

SUBJECT

IDEAS

PICTURES/GRAPHICS

ROUGH DRAFT

NOTES

OTHER

MY BLOG IDEAS
MIND MAP

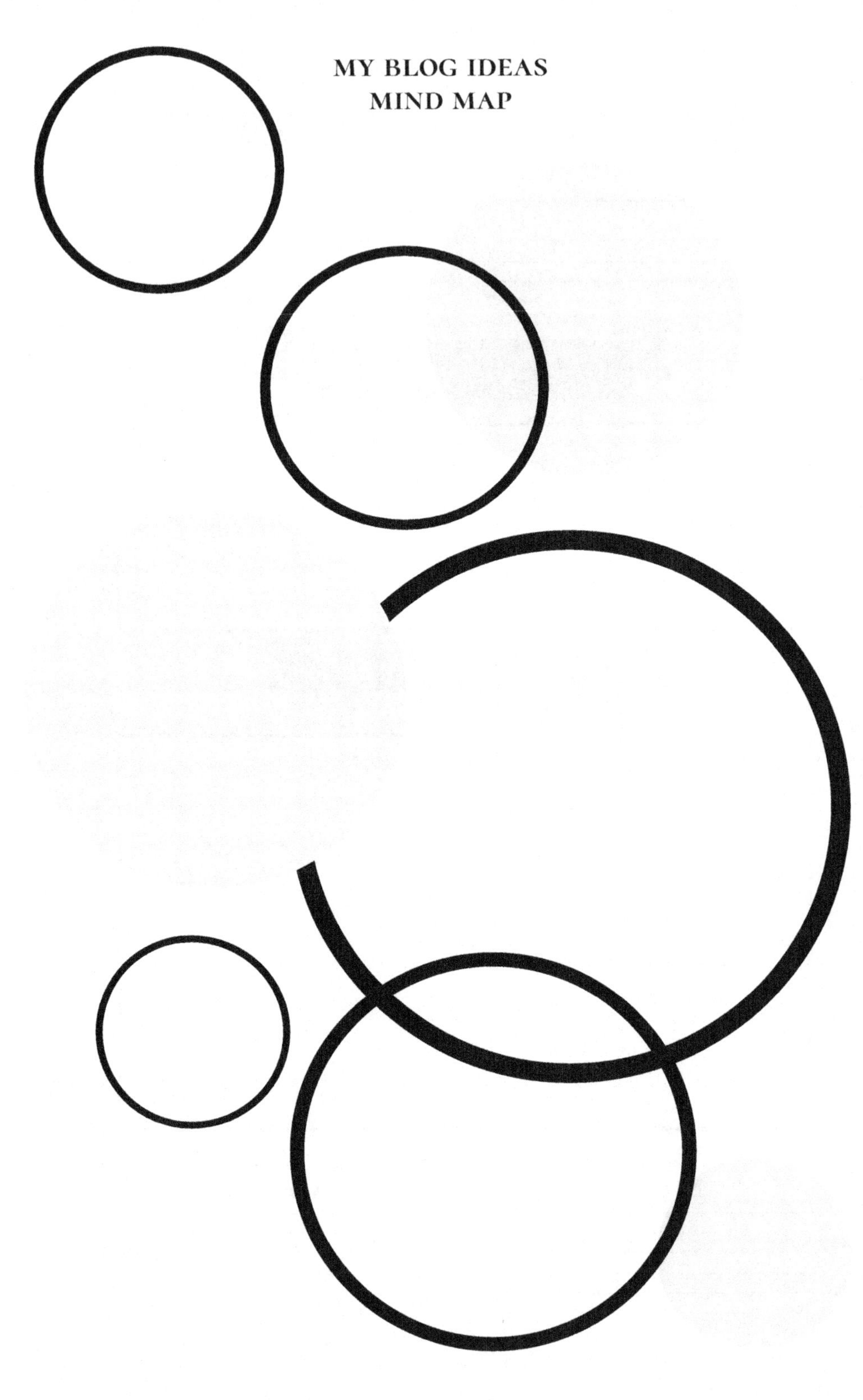

MY BLOG IDEAS

SUBJECT

IDEAS

PICTURES/GRAPHICS

ROUGH DRAFT

NOTES

OTHER

MY BLOG IDEAS MIND MAP

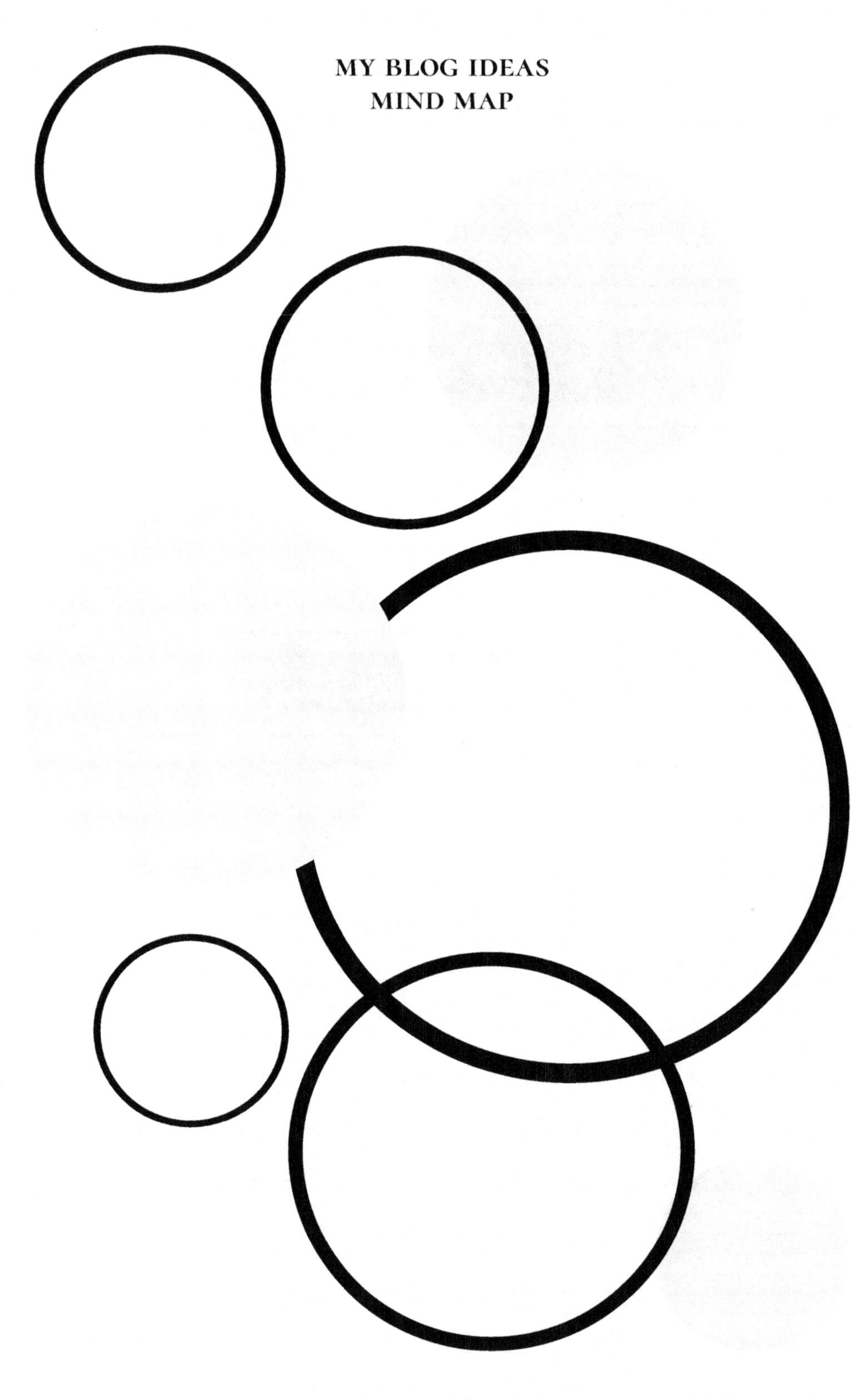

MY BLOG IDEAS

SUBJECT

IDEAS

PICTURES/GRAPHICS

ROUGH DRAFT

NOTES

OTHER

MY BLOG IDEAS MIND MAP

MY BLOG IDEAS

SUBJECT

IDEAS

PICTURES/GRAPHICS

ROUGH DRAFT

NOTES

OTHER

MY BLOG IDEAS
MIND MAP

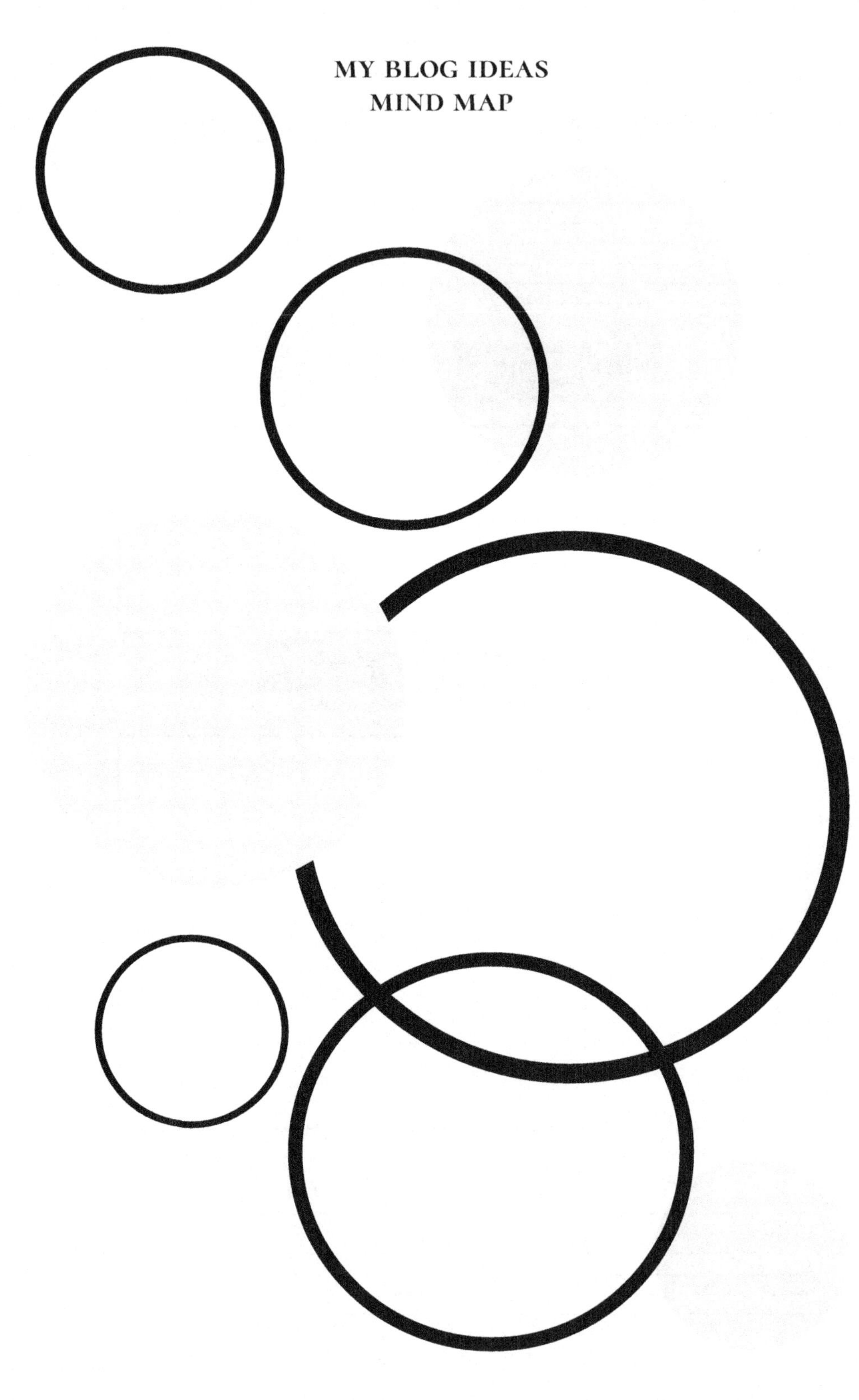

MY BLOG IDEAS

SUBJECT

IDEAS

PICTURES/GRAPHICS

ROUGH DRAFT

NOTES

OTHER

MY BLOG IDEAS MIND MAP

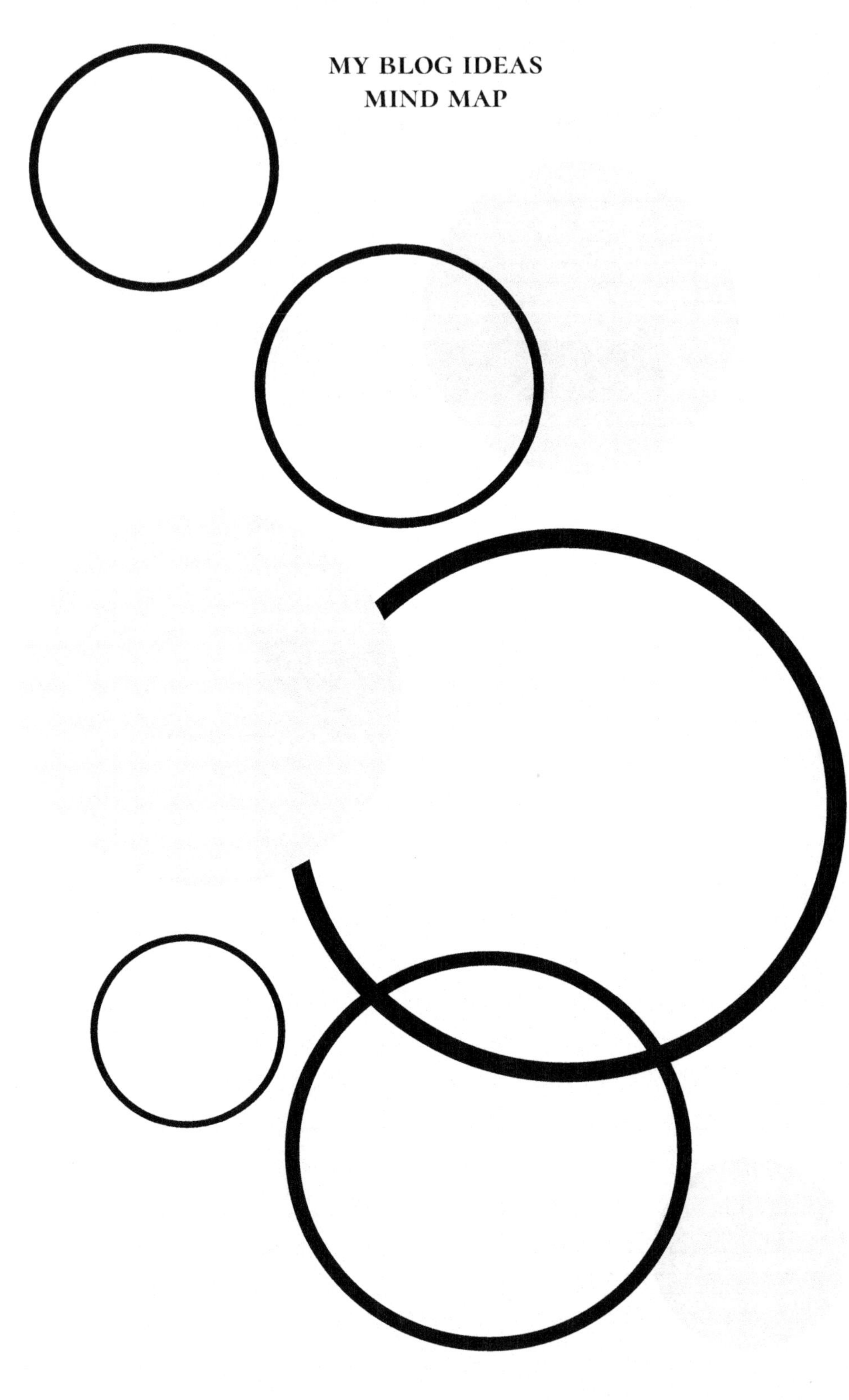

MY BLOG IDEAS

SUBJECT

IDEAS

PICTURES/GRAPHICS

ROUGH DRAFT

NOTES

OTHER

MY BLOG IDEAS
MIND MAP

MY BLOG IDEAS

SUBJECT

IDEAS

PICTURES/GRAPHICS

ROUGH DRAFT

NOTES

OTHER

MY BLOG IDEAS MIND MAP

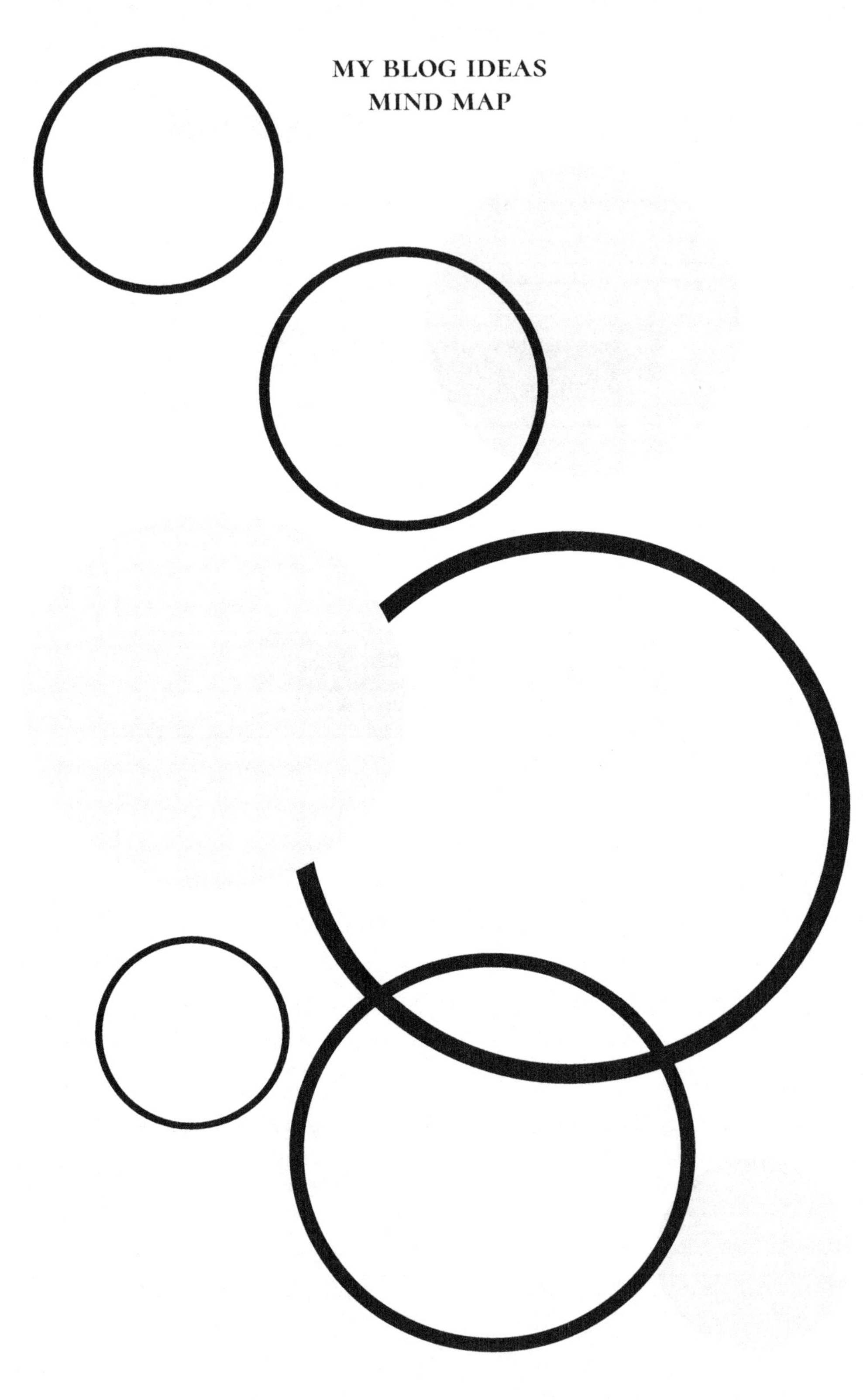

MY BLOG IDEAS

SUBJECT

IDEAS

PICTURES/GRAPHICS

ROUGH DRAFT

NOTES

OTHER

MY BLOG IDEAS MIND MAP

MY BLOG IDEAS

SUBJECT

IDEAS

PICTURES/GRAPHICS

ROUGH DRAFT

NOTES

OTHER

MY BLOG IDEAS
MIND MAP

MY BLOG IDEAS

SUBJECT

IDEAS

PICTURES/GRAPHICS

ROUGH DRAFT

NOTES

OTHER

MY BLOG IDEAS MIND MAP

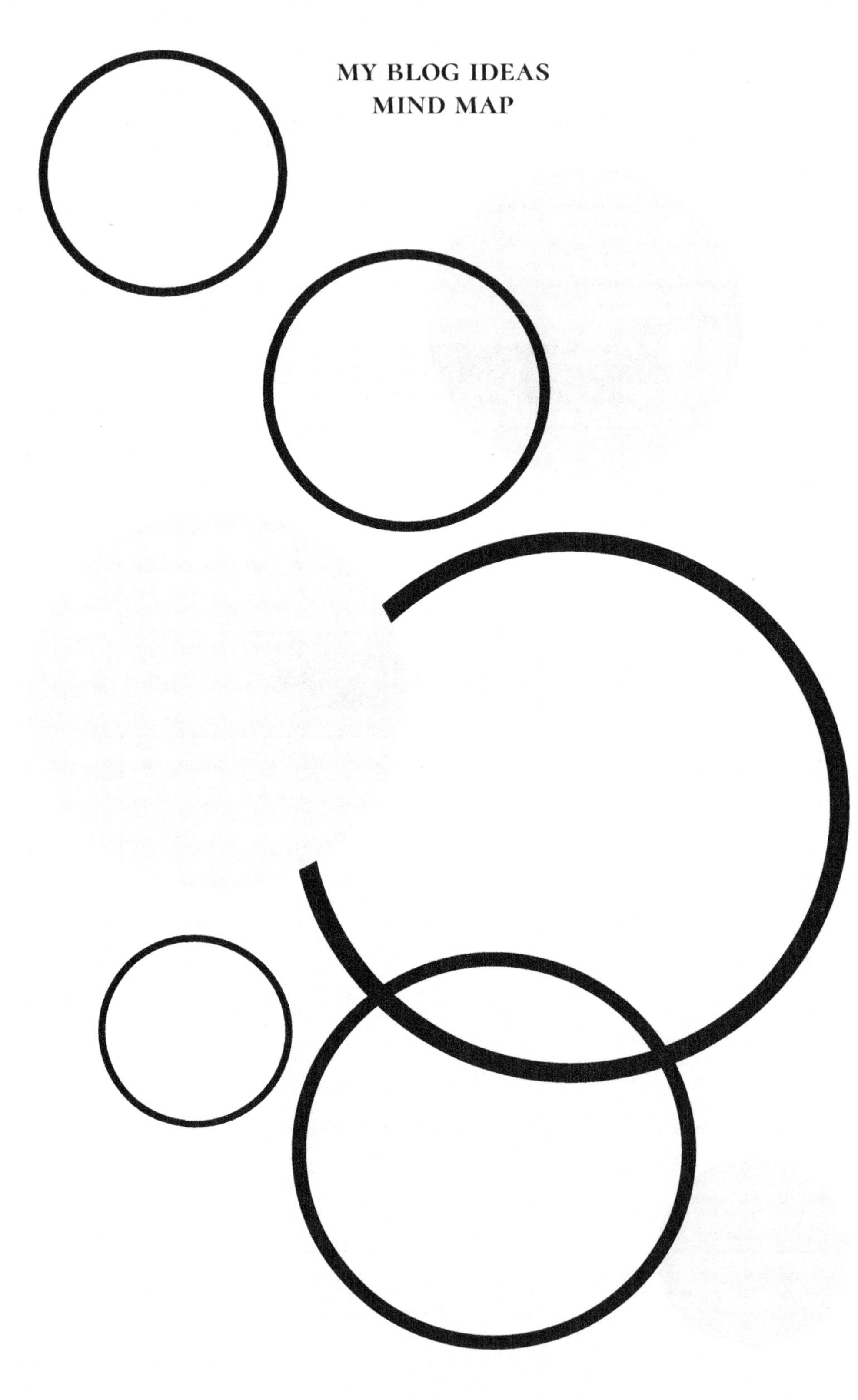

MY BLOG IDEAS

SUBJECT

IDEAS

PICTURES/GRAPHICS

ROUGH DRAFT

NOTES

OTHER

MY BLOG IDEAS
MIND MAP

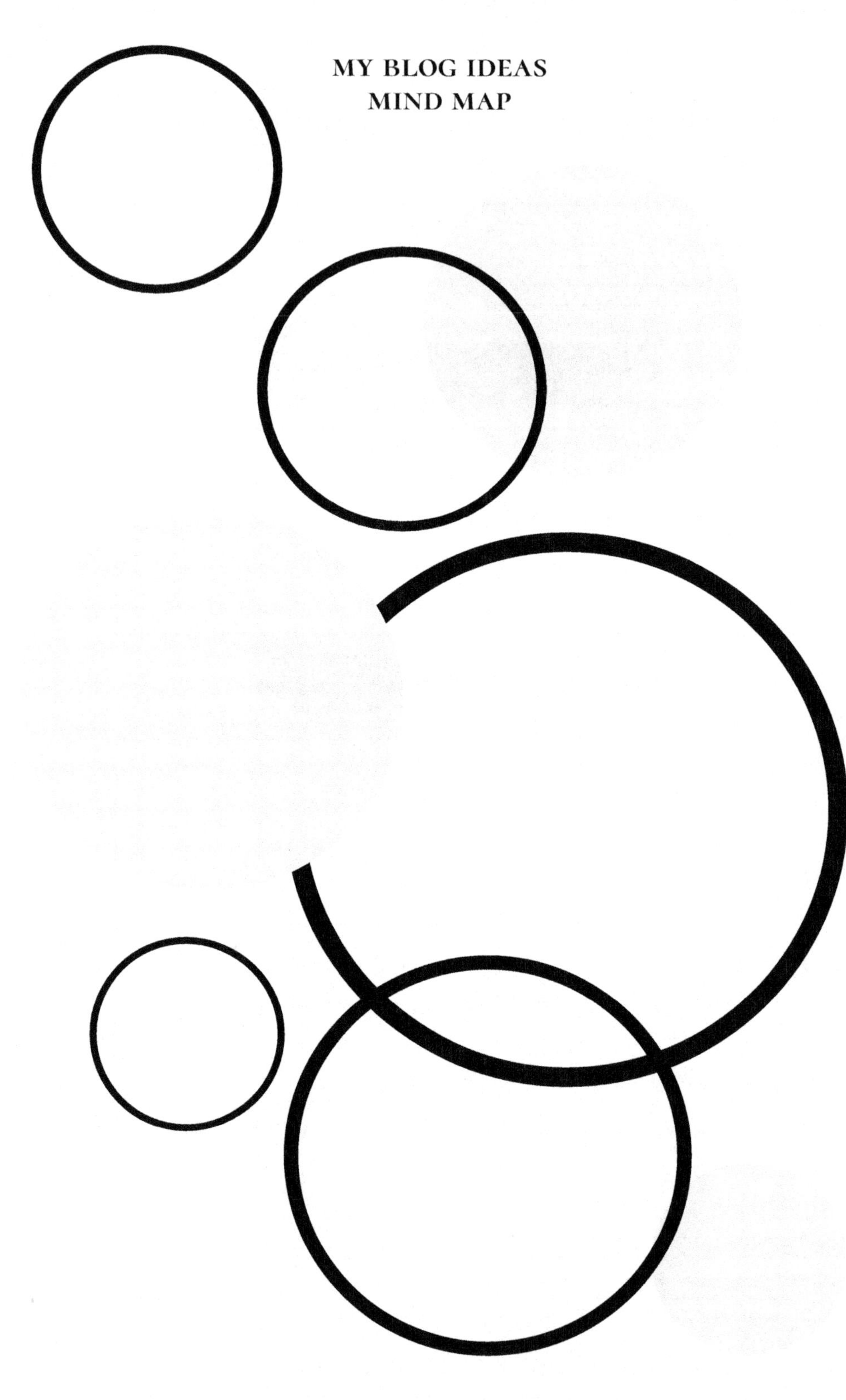

MY BLOG IDEAS

SUBJECT

IDEAS

PICTURES/GRAPHICS

ROUGH DRAFT

NOTES

OTHER

MY BLOG IDEAS
MIND MAP

MY BLOG IDEAS

SUBJECT

IDEAS

PICTURES/GRAPHICS

ROUGH DRAFT

NOTES

OTHER

MY BLOG IDEAS
MIND MAP

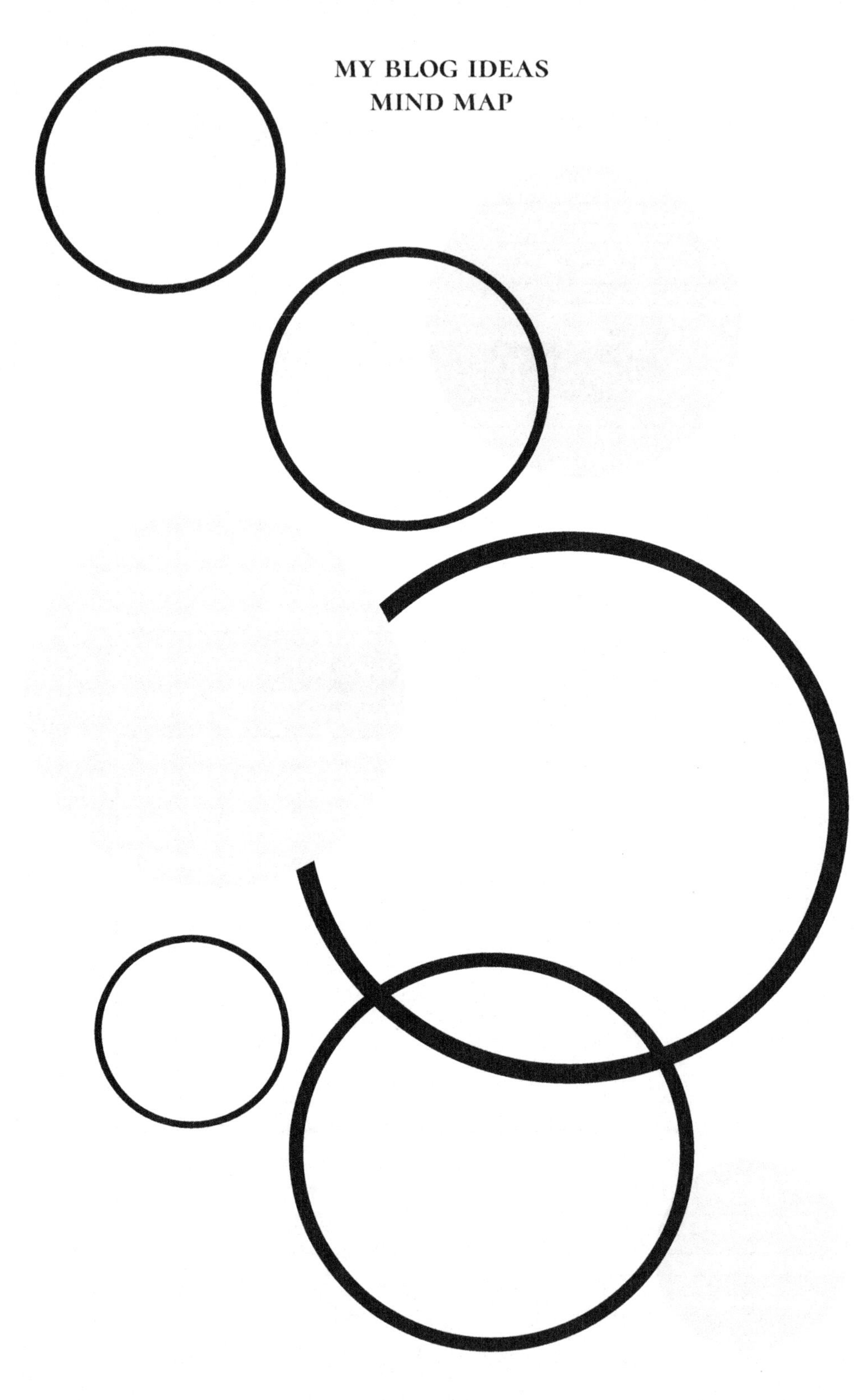

MY BLOG IDEAS

SUBJECT

IDEAS

PICTURES/GRAPHICS

ROUGH DRAFT

NOTES

OTHER

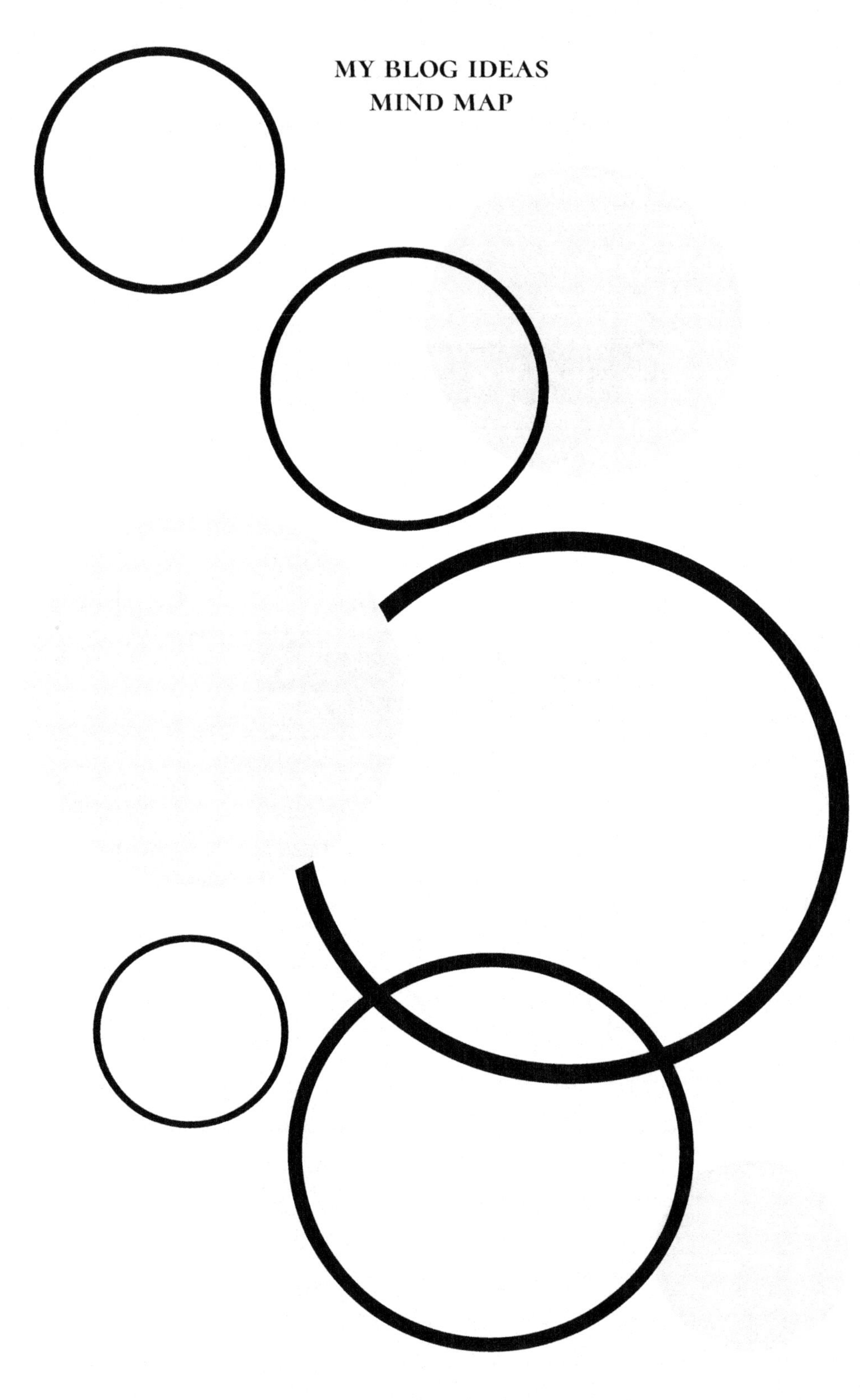
MY BLOG IDEAS
MIND MAP

MY BLOG IDEAS

SUBJECT

IDEAS

PICTURES/GRAPHICS

ROUGH DRAFT

NOTES

OTHER

MY BLOG IDEAS MIND MAP

MY BLOG IDEAS

SUBJECT

IDEAS

PICTURES/GRAPHICS

ROUGH DRAFT

NOTES

OTHER

MY BLOG IDEAS
MIND MAP

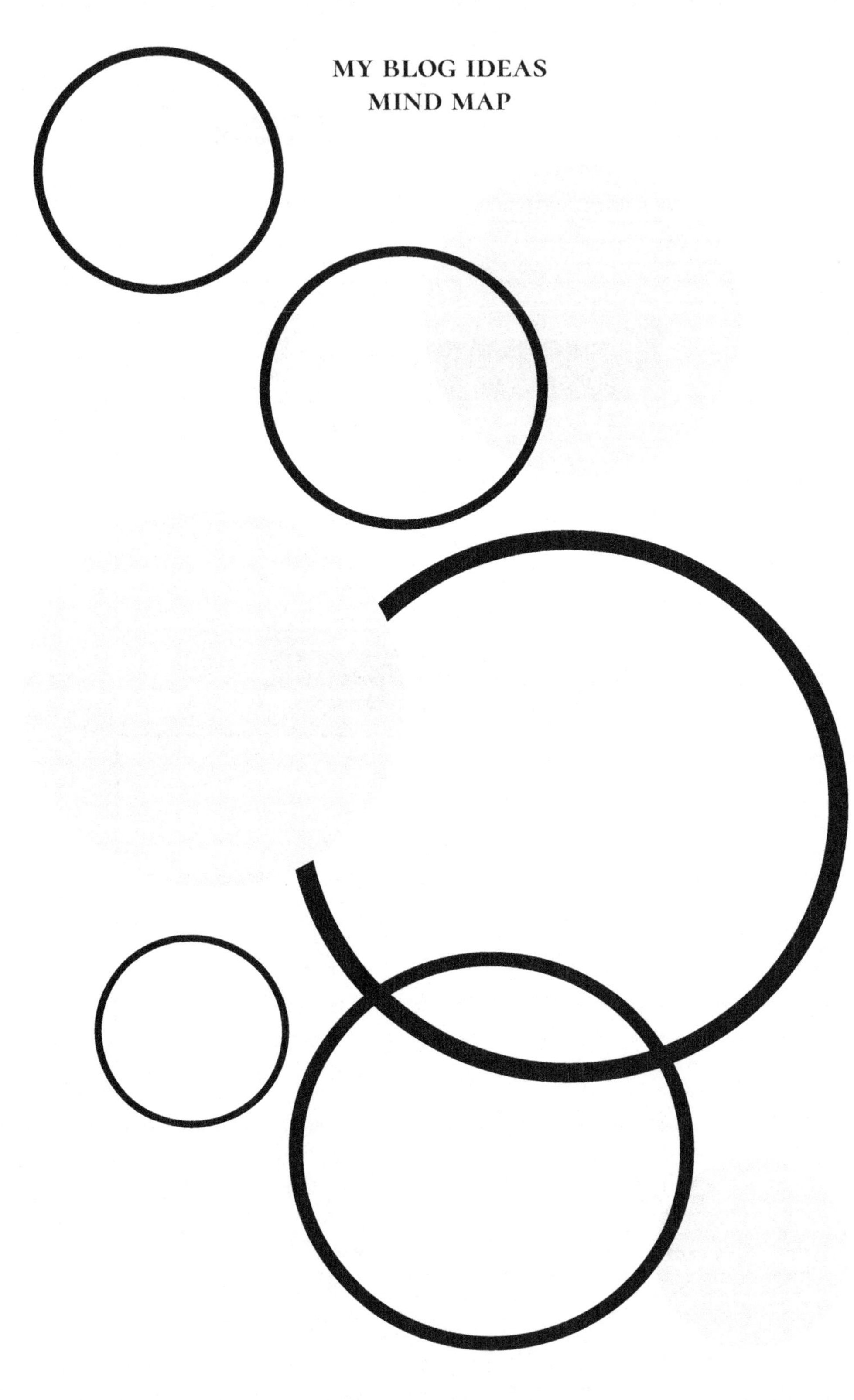

MY BLOG IDEAS

SUBJECT

IDEAS

PICTURES/GRAPHICS

ROUGH DRAFT

NOTES

OTHER

MY BLOG IDEAS
MIND MAP

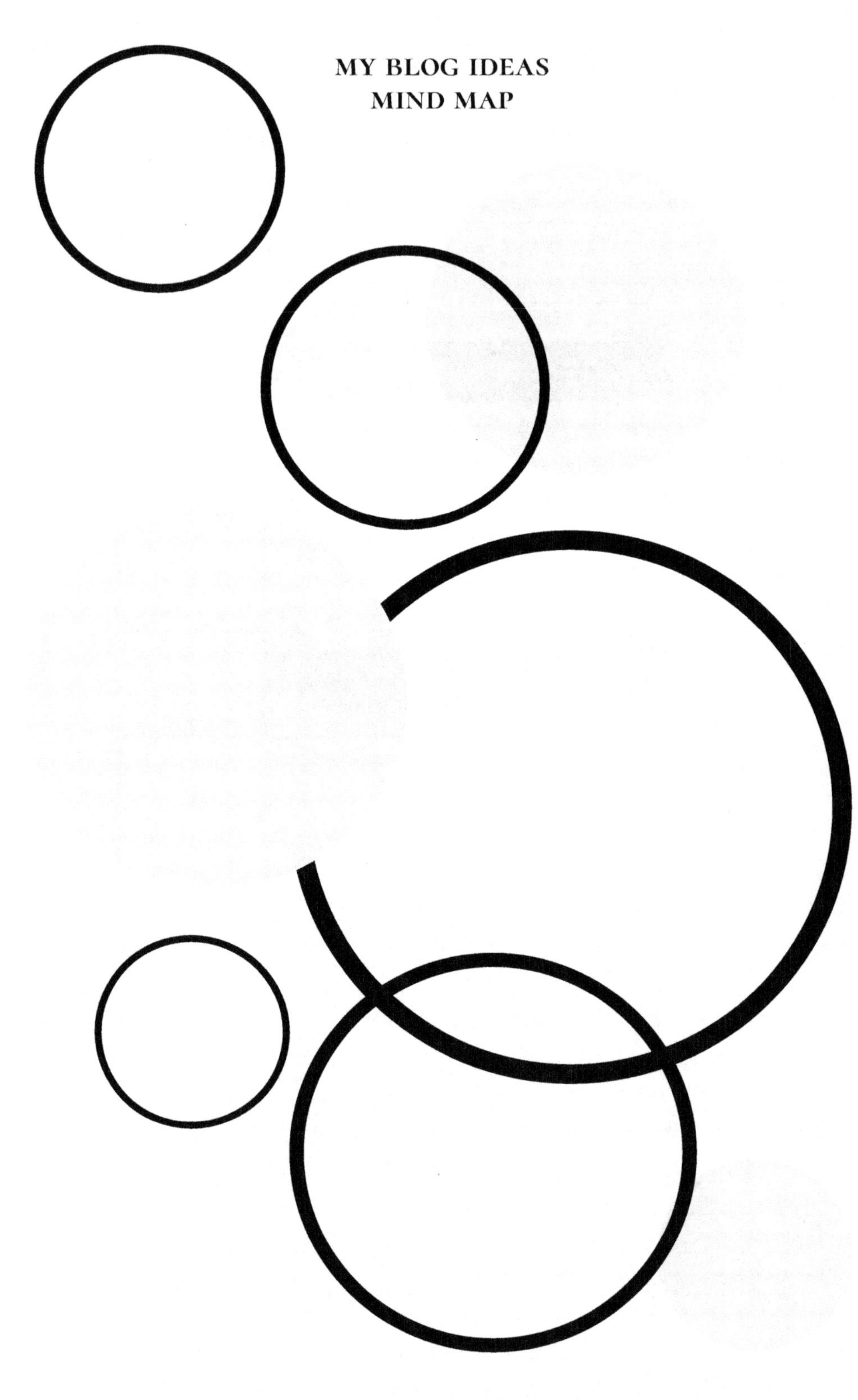

MY BLOG IDEAS

SUBJECT

IDEAS

PICTURES/GRAPHICS

ROUGH DRAFT

NOTES

OTHER

MY BLOG IDEAS MIND MAP

MY BLOG IDEAS

SUBJECT

IDEAS

PICTURES/GRAPHICS

ROUGH DRAFT

NOTES

OTHER

MY BLOG IDEAS
MIND MAP

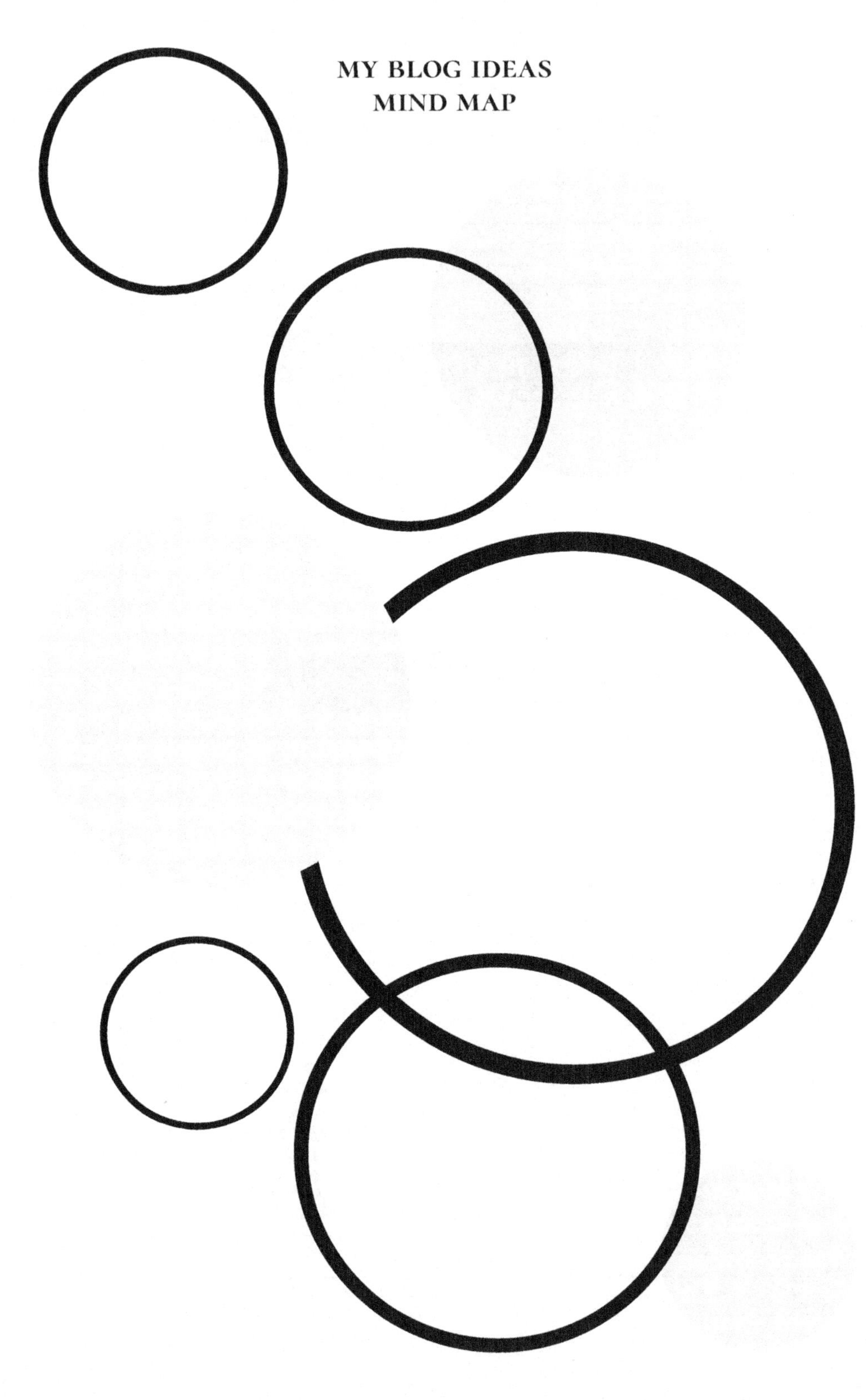

MY BLOG IDEAS

SUBJECT

IDEAS

PICTURES/GRAPHICS

ROUGH DRAFT

NOTES

OTHER

MY BLOG IDEAS
MIND MAP

MY BLOG IDEAS

SUBJECT

IDEAS

PICTURES/GRAPHICS

ROUGH DRAFT

NOTES

OTHER

MY BLOG IDEAS MIND MAP

MY BLOG IDEAS

SUBJECT

IDEAS

PICTURES/GRAPHICS

ROUGH DRAFT

NOTES

OTHER

MY BLOG IDEAS MIND MAP

MY BLOG IDEAS

SUBJECT

IDEAS

PICTURES/GRAPHICS

ROUGH DRAFT

NOTES

OTHER

MY BLOG IDEAS
MIND MAP

MY BLOG IDEAS

SUBJECT

IDEAS

PICTURES/GRAPHICS

ROUGH DRAFT

NOTES

OTHER

MY BLOG IDEAS
MIND MAP

MY BLOG IDEAS

SUBJECT

IDEAS

PICTURES/GRAPHICS

ROUGH DRAFT

NOTES

OTHER

MY BLOG IDEAS MIND MAP

MY BLOG IDEAS

SUBJECT

IDEAS

PICTURES/GRAPHICS

ROUGH DRAFT

NOTES

OTHER

Printed in Great Britain
by Amazon

21931438R00069